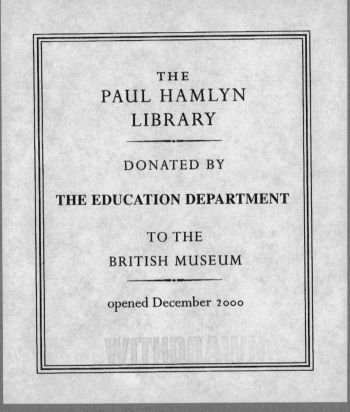

First published 1975
Reprinted 1977, 1978,
    1980, 1981
Macdonald Educational
Holywell House
Worship Street
London EC2A 2EN

© Macdonald Educational
Limited 1975

ISBN 0 356 05108 0
(cased edition)
ISBN 0 356 06503 0
(limp edition)

Made and printed by
Interlitho s.p.a.
Italy

Editor
Verity Weston

Design
Sarah Tyzack

Editorial Assistant
Julia Kirk

Production
Philip Hughes

Illustrators
Peter Connolly
Ron Hayward Associates
Angus McBride/Faulkner
Marks
Peter North
Tony Payne
Peter Thornley

Consultants
Harry Strongman
Senior Lecturer in History,
Berkshire College of
Education

Dr I. E. S. Edwards
Formerly Keeper of
Egyptian Antiquities,
British Museum

Photographs
Sarah Tyzack: 19(B), 28, 39, 41(B)
Michael Holford: 26, 48
Roger Wood: 8, 11, 31, 47(T), 54, 55
Verity Weston: 37, 41(T)
Lehnert & Landrock: 46

F. L. Kenett/George Rainbird: 22
William Macquitty: 19(T), 47(B)
Spectrum: 18
British Museum: 45
Ashmolean Museum: 36
Glasgow Museum: 34

The Egyptians

Anne Millard

Macdonald Educational

The Egyptians

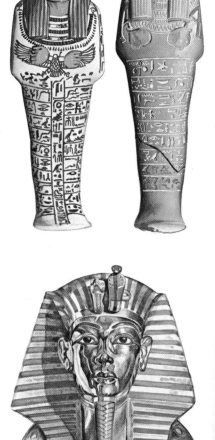

Egypt was not only one of the very earliest of the great civilizations of the world. It also survived, relatively unchanged, longer than almost any other.

The Egyptians developed a way of life that suited their surroundings perfectly. They formed a set of ideas and beliefs that contented them for more than 3000 years. Today, in museums all over the world, we look a little enviously at their statues, which gaze into eternity with such serene confidence.

There are very few ancient Egyptian towns available to excavate. Many of them are buried, deep under modern cities. The rest have decayed and the bricks from which they were built have long ago become one with the Nile mud, from which they came. Only rarely, such as at Tell el Amarna, do we find a site to excavate.

This is unfortunate, but we have much to make up for this lack. There are the great stone temples and pyramids, which are so impressive in their size and grandeur that no photograph ever does them justice. There are the tombs, whose walls are decorated with scenes of daily life so vivid that you half expect to see them move.

Every metre of land in Egypt was needed to grow crops so burials took place in the desert or in the cliffs. The Egyptians put in their tombs everything they would need in the next world. Because of the dry climate, these things were preserved. Even after thousands of years, we can actually handle their personal possessions.

Also, because we understand hieroglyphs, we can hear the echo of the Egyptians' voices, speaking to us through their books, letters and inscriptions. It is worth taking the time to listen.

Contents

"Egypt is the gift of the Nile"

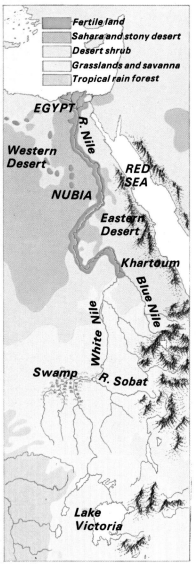

Fertile land
Sahara and stony desert
Desert shrub
Grasslands and savanna
Tropical rain forest

EGYPT

R. Nile

Western Desert

RED SEA

NUBIA

Eastern Desert

Khartoum

Blue Nile

White Nile

Swamp R. Sobat

Lake Victoria

▲ The Nile is formed when the White Nile, which rises in the lakes of central Africa, meets the Blue Nile from the mountains of Ethiopia. Without the Nile Egypt would be a desert, just like the rest of the Sahara.

There is very little rain, and most of it falls in the northern part of the country and only in the winter months.

The words above were written some 2,300 years ago, by the great Greek historian Herodotus, in his famous book on Egypt. They are as true today as they were then. To understand the story of Egypt, we must first understand the ways of its river.

The river Nile was once much wider than it is now and it flowed across a vast, flat plain. Over the centuries the river shrank in width, cutting its channel deeper and deeper. In some places it cut down through rock, leaving behind steep cliffs, where nothing could grow. Elsewhere it uncovered flat, fertile stretches of land, just right for farming.

The valley that was formed was never more than a few kilometres wide, even at its widest point. Every metre of land was therefore precious and had to be carefully used. The river only divides north of Cairo, seeking its way to the sea through many channels. Thus it forms the triangular-shaped area of good farming land known as the Delta.

Once a year, melting snows and heavy rains in the Ethiopian mountains send a great torrent of water and mud crashing down the Blue Nile into the Nile. Until the building of modern dams, so much water surged down the Nile that it overflowed. The whole land was flooded, right down to the Mediterranean Sea. This was known as the Inundation. When the Inundation went down, it covered the land with a new layer of rich, black soil, which was damp enough to grow crops.

The Inundation

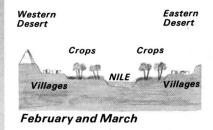

February and March

August and September

▲ Each year the Inundation covered the land on either side of the river. But there was never the same amount of water. Too much meant that houses would be flooded and men and animals might drown. Too little water meant that the crops would die and there would be famine until after the next Inundation.

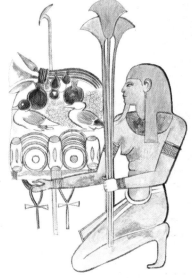

▲ This ancient Egyptian painting is of Hapi, the Nile god. He provided water to drink and for crops; fish and wild fowl to eat; and reeds to make into many useful things.

"Hail to you O Nile, who issues from the

▲ Nobles hunted water birds for sport, using a throwing stick to bring them down, and a trained cat to retrieve them.

Above is the first line of a hymn to Hapi, the Nile god. It tells of all the god's many gifts to mankind. It must have been very popular as many copies have survived. Most of them were written by schoolboys during their lessons. Their spelling often has mistakes in it.

The fish that lived in the Nile, and the birds that lived in the reeds along its banks were valuable sources of food. Men fishing for food worked in teams with large nets, but a nobleman would fish alone for sport, using a spear. His boat would be a small, frail craft, made of bundles of papyrus lashed together. This could easily be overturned by a hippopotamus!

Scenes in tombs show how fowlers hid nets among the reeds, tempting the unwary birds in with bait. When enough birds had been lured in, the men pulled on the ropes and the net snapped shut over the birds.

▲ Not all Hapi's creatures were pleasant or useful. Crocodiles and hippopotami made the river dangerous.

earth and comes to keep Egypt alive"

▲ Papyrus stems were used to make mats, baskets, furniture, sandals, paper, boats and roofs of houses.

▲ Fishermen worked in teams. They cast large nets into the water, while they stood in small boats or on the river bank.

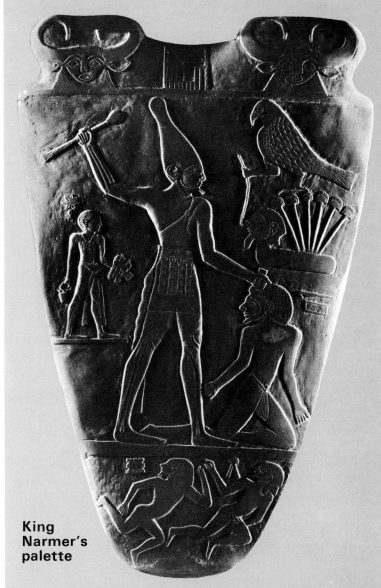

King Narmer's palette

The early settlers needed great courage to enter the Nile Valley, with its dangerous marshes and animals. Their descendants slowly found new ways of living as herdsmen and farmers. To succeed, they had to learn how to irrigate the land by storing the Nile waters in a system of canals. This meant that they had to work together, and they needed strong, clever leaders. Gradually, their small settlements were united by alliance or conquest.

The ceremonial palette above, used for mixing eye paint, belonged to Narmer. He may have been the king who united Egypt. After the Unification, cities grew up, but most people continued to be farmers.

Ships of the Nile

The cultivated, inhabited part of Egypt is long and very narrow, with the Nile flowing through it. So in the days before railways and cars, the quickest and easiest way to travel and to transport heavy loads was by boats of all sizes.

When a journey was needed, the Egyptians always thought of boats. Even the sun god, Ra, was believed to sail across the sky every day in a barge on a Nile in the sky. Archaeologists have found a barge buried for one king, for his use in the next world.

The Nile flows from south to north, but the wind in Egypt usually blows from north to south. A sailor travelling northwards would therefore have the current with him. This would make rowing easier, but he would hardly ever be able to use his sails. On the return journey the wind would be with him, so he could sail. But if the wind dropped, he would have a hard time rowing against the current.

Ships were steered by special oars at the stern. Ships varied in size from small reed boats to great merchant ships and warships. The elegant barges built for the king and the nobles, or to carry the statues of the gods, were gaily painted and gilded. They had comfortable cabins and bright sails.

▼ A stone obelisk from the granite quarries of southern Egypt is carried to Thebes by barge. The flat-bottomed barge is so huge that it has to be towed by many small boats.

Some small boats, for use on the river only, were made of papyrus. The others, especially sea-going vessels, were made of wood.

Large trees did not grow in Egypt so wood had to be imported, usually from the Lebanon.

The farmer's year

▲ **1**. Every year, some time in July, the level of the water in the Nile began to rise. This was the beginning of the Inundation.

▶ **2**. When the land was flooded, the farmers had little to do, so many of them worked for the Pharaoh on one of his building projects.

▲ **3**. By November the water had gone down. Farmers got to work quickly. Heavy soil was broken up to make ploughing easier.

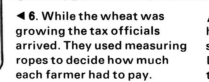

◀ **6**. While the wheat was growing the tax officials arrived. They used measuring ropes to decide how much each farmer had to pay.

▲ **7**. By the end of March the harvest was in, reaped with sickles with flint blades. Donkeys carried the corn to the threshing floor.

▼ 4. The fields were ploughed, the furrows hoed. The sowers scattered the seed, which animals trod deep into the rich, damp soil.

► 5. Water had to be let into the irrigation canals, little by little. There was always weeding to be done as the crops grew.

◄ 8. Cattle were driven across the wheat to separate the grain from the husk. Women tossed the grain in the wind to remove the husks.

▲ 9. The grain was then stored. By now it was getting very hot and the farmers started to wait anxiously for the next Inundation.

Cooking, eating and drinking

▲ Egyptian women usually prepared meals outside. Scientists have analyzed ancient loaves and found a lot of grit in them. This might have blown in while the loaves were being prepared.

Bread and beer were basic items in the Egyptian diet. To make bread, the housewife had to get grain from her granary and grind it into flour between two stones. This was very hard work. She mixed the flour with water and made it into loaves of many shapes and sizes. Sometimes she might add a flavouring, such as garlic.

If the housewife wanted to make beer, she would bake her loaves very lightly. She would then crumble them, mix them with water and leave the mixture to ferment and so become beer. The mixture had to be strained before it was ready for drinking.

The Egyptians raised cattle, sheep and goats and enjoyed eating the meat that came from them. Everyone ate lots of vegetables, especially leeks, beans, radishes, cucumbers and lettuces. The Egyptians also made cheese. There was no sugar in the ancient world, so they used honey to sweeten things.

Cooking was done over an open fire, so meat had to be roasted on spits or stewed in cooking pots. The bread was baked in pottery containers placed round the fire.

This painting shows two men using trained baboons to help them pick figs. Besides figs, the Egyptians enjoyed pomegranates, dates and grapes.

The Egyptians trained their vines to grow over wooden trellises. When the grapes were ripe they were picked and placed in a stone trough, where men trampled on them to extract the juice. The juice ran out through a funnel and was caught and put in wine jars. The men left the jars open until the wine had fermented. Then they sealed the jars with mud stoppers. Besides wine and beer, the Egyptians drank milk and, of course, water.

▲ This Egyptian tomb painting shows men picking grapes to make wine.

▲ The Egyptians believed that the dead needed food as much as the living, so they put it in tombs. Thanks to the very dry climate, some of this has survived to the present day.

▶ This model from a tomb shows a butcher at work. Beef was a favourite dish of the Egyptians. They also raised sheep, ducks, geese and pigeons and caught fish, gazelles and birds.

Houses of farmers and workmen

▼ This reconstruction of a medium-sized house in the country is based on pottery models called "soul houses", which were sometimes put in tombs. The family would spend a lot of time on the roof to catch the breeze and escape from the stifling heat below.

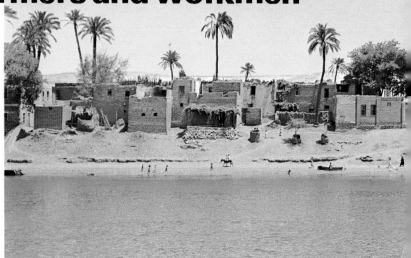

▲ The shaduf was known in ancient Egypt too. It is used to raise water from one level to another.

Houses of reeds, mud and wood

The smallest, poorest Egyptian houses were probably made from reeds, wood and mud. They might have had only one room, and probably were not very comfortable. But they gave some shelter against cold nights and sand storms.

All other houses, even palaces, were made of mud bricks. Workmen mixed the rich, sticky Nile mud with sand or chopped straw to get it to the right consistency. They usually put the ingredients in a pit and mixed them by stamping up and down. The mud was then shaped in rectangular moulds and dried out in the hot sun.

Columns and roofs would be of wood, but column bases and door steps and posts might be stone. In larger houses, the walls were plastered and brightly painted. Windows were small and placed near the ceiling, but the sunlight was so bright that enough light got in.

Workmen's houses at Tell el Amarna

The small houses of the workmen at Tell el Amarna had no gardens, but they had the same basic divisions as the large villas. The outer room opened on to the street. This was where visitors entered and where the man of the house might work, if he were a craftsman.

The central hall was the main living area, where friends were invited and entertained. At the back was a small bedroom, a kitchen and a staircase to the roof. Women and children spent much of their time on the roof, where it was cooler. A small kiosk or a canopy sheltered them from the sun. Cooking was often done outside the house, because this reduced the risk of fire.

▲ The ancient method of making bricks of mud was so satisfactory that it is still in use today.

A nobleman's villa

▼ An artist's reconstruction of a villa at Tell el Amarna.

In towns, land was scarce. The houses were therefore tall, narrow and crowded together. Some were three or four storeys high. But in the country, where there was plenty of room, rich Egyptians built large and beautiful villas in shady gardens. They built high walls around them to stop people looking in.

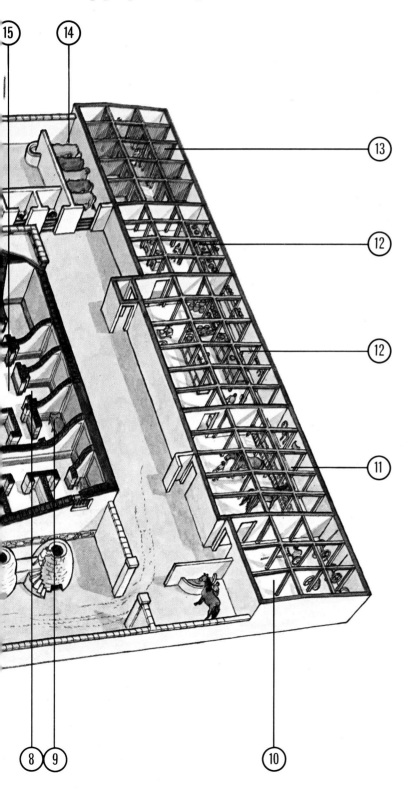

1. The porter's lodge.

2. The family chapel.

3. Main entrance.

4. Entrance to house.

5. Reception room. Houses had three main areas. The front of the house contained rooms where business was conducted and visitors were received.

6. The central hall. This was in the second group of rooms, where the family entertained their friends. The hall was taller than all the rooms around it and had windows high up in the walls.

7. Grain silos. Every house stored the grain from which bread and beer were made.

8. One of the bedrooms. It is situated in the third area of the house, the family's private living quarters.

9. Bathroom, with stone slabs lining walls and floors, and a lavatory.

10. Chariot house.

11. Stables.

12. Kitchens.

13. Servants' quarters and store rooms.

14. Cattle pens.

15. The family's private living room.

16. One of the many store rooms.

17. One of the rooms on the upper floor.

18. Well.

19. Garden.

20. Garden pool.

Inside the home

The interiors of poor peasants' houses were simple, with very little furniture. But the houses of richer people were often beautifully decorated and furnished.

People who could afford them had wooden beds, tables, chairs, stools and storage chests of all shapes and sizes. The seats of chairs and stools were often made of leather or reeds. Luxury furniture was made of rich woods such as ebony and cedar.

People ate with their fingers. Most people used plates, dishes and cups of pottery. Some had vessels made of a blue glazed material called faience. In the tombs of some members of the royal family, however, vessels of gold and silver have been found.

Egyptians loved parties. At a rich man's banquet there was always a lot to eat and drink. Flowers decorated the room and small cones of perfume were placed on the guests' heads. Dancers, acrobats, singers and musicians entertained the guests. Harps, flutes and lutes were favourite instruments. Here, one musician also beats a leather percussion instrument.

▲ The magnificent throne of Tutankhamun. It is covered with gold and inlaid with silver and semi-precious stones.

Clothes, cosmetics and jewels

Beauty aids

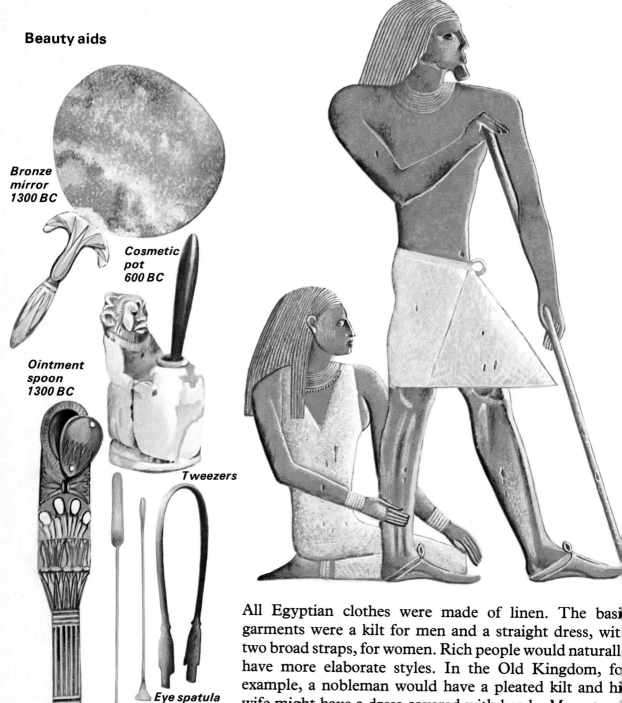

Bronze
mirror
1300 BC

Cosmetic
pot
600 BC

Ointment
spoon
1300 BC

Tweezers

Eye spatula

Cosmetic scoop

Comb

All Egyptian clothes were made of linen. The basi
garments were a kilt for men and a straight dress, wit
two broad straps, for women. Rich people would naturall
have more elaborate styles. In the Old Kingdom, fo
example, a nobleman would have a pleated kilt and hi
wife might have a dress covered with beads. Many tom
paintings show people in white clothes, but they ha
coloured cloth too.

For ceremonies and special occasions men and wome
wore heavy wigs. Both sexes used cosmetics. The mos
important items in a cosmetic box were the oils used t
stop the skin drying up in the hot sun. Kohl, used to pai
the eyes, and perfumes were also very important.

Jewellery

▲ An elaborate pendant hung on a string of beads is called a pectoral.

▲ Both these lovely pectorals belonged to King Tutankhamun and were found in his tomb.

▲ This golden bracelet of Tutankhamun has a scarab beetle carved on it.

By the New Kingdom, costumes had become much more elaborate. Both men and women wore robes of draped and pleated linen. Egypt has a very pleasant climate, so warm cloaks were only needed for a short time in the winter, and then mainly in the north. In summer most children, and adults who were doing heavy work, did not bother to wear any clothes at all.

Everyone, whatever their age or sex, wore lots of jewellery. They had circlets for their heads, earrings, necklaces of many kinds, rings, bracelets and anklets. The materials ranged from gold, silver and semi-precious stones to glazed beads, shells and polished pebbles of attractive colours.

Fun and games

▼ This painting is from the tomb of a nobleman. It shows him and his family enjoying a day out on the river. The nobleman is hunting birds with a throwing stick. Another man is held steady by his wife while he spears fish.

▲ Egyptians of all ages enjoyed games of skill or chance. The rules have been lost, but they probably resembled games like chess, draughts and ludo.

▲ This gaming board belonged to Tutankhamun. It was put in his tomb so that he could play in the next world.

People tend to think that the Egyptians were sad and solemn because they spent so much time preparing for death. This is not true. Of course they had their serious side, but they loved this life so much that they wanted the next world to be just like it.

There were plenty of indoor games to amuse people. But energetic young noblemen preferred to be out in their chariots hunting, or on the river, fishing, fowling or chasing hippopotami and crocodiles.

Wrestling and swimming were popular. There was also another sport, which resembled fencing, except that the men used sticks. Boatmen used to form teams and hold competitions on the river. They were armed with poles and the aim was to push your opponents into the water!

Some children's toys have survived in the dry sand of Egypt. Dolls and leather balls seem to have been especially popular. Pictures in tombs also show children dancing and playing team games and leap-frog.

There were no theatres, but religious processions and military parades gave the Egyptians the chance to see magnificent shows.

▲ These two young men appear in a tomb painting from Thebes. They have been out for a day's sport on the river.

▲ Egyptian children loved toy animals. The lion snaps his jaw when you jerk the string.

▲ This wooden horse on wheels was the prize possession of one small child.

Descendants of the gods

The title Pharaoh comes from two ancient Egyptian words: "per aa", meaning "the Great House", that is the palace. The kings of Egypt were supposed to be descended from the gods, so it was not respectful to refer directly to the king doing something. Instead you had to say "the Great House has done this".

In the distant past, Egypt had been two kingdoms. These were united by a king called Menes, but the memory of the two lands was always preserved in the title "King of Upper and Lower Egypt". Kings were crowned with the crowns of Upper and Lower Egypt.

It was the duty of the king to keep the two lands united by serving the gods and governing according to their laws. To assist him in this mighty task the king had an army of ministers, officials and scribes. The chief minister was the Vizier.

The Colossi of Memnon on the west bank of the Nile at Thebes. These huge statues are all that is now left of the magnificent temple built by King Amenhotep III.

A pharaoh's life

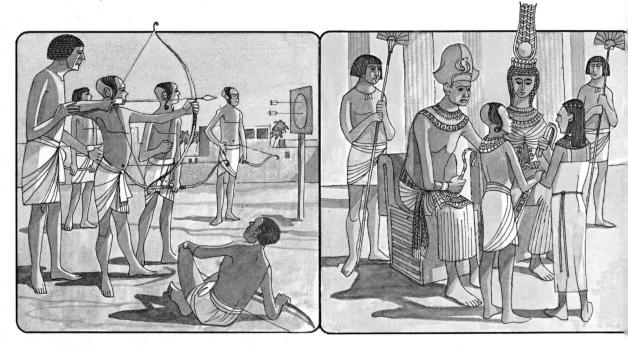

▲ In the days before modern medicines, many children died young. It was therefore necessary for all the young princes to be carefully trained, in case they had to be king one day, instead of the chosen heir.

▲ Pharaohs had one queen but several minor wives. The son of the queen was the official heir. He would marry his sister because he was descended from the gods and no one else was great enough to become his queen.

▲ It was the king's duty to care for the well-being of his subjects, according to the will of the gods. One of his important duties was tending the irrigation system. Here he supervizes the opening of a new canal.

▲ Besides being a law-giver, administrator and priest, the Pharaoh also had to be a skilled warrior. It was his task to protect his people against their enemies and to defend the frontiers of the kingdom.

▶ The sky god Horus sometimes chose to appear as a hawk. Here he protects the young prince who was to become Ramesses II.

▲ When the king sat on his throne, wearing his regalia, the spirit of Horus was said to enter him. The king then became divine too. He was the living link between men and the gods and his every word had to be obeyed.

▲ At death, the Pharaoh was buried in a magnificent tomb. Paintings in it showed the king being received into the kingdom of Osiris, the god of the dead. There the Pharaoh would become a god too and live for ever.

Soldiers, weapons and war

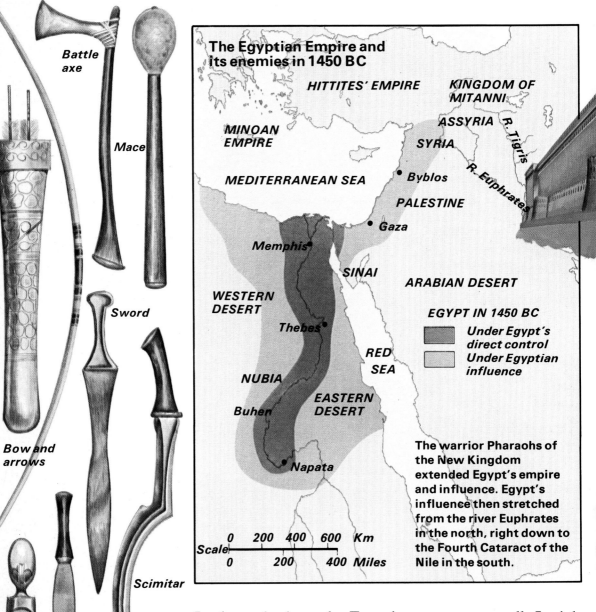

Battle axe

Mace

Sword

Bow and arrows

Scimitar

Daggers

The Egyptian Empire and its enemies in 1450 BC

HITTITES' EMPIRE

KINGDOM OF MITANNI

MINOAN EMPIRE

ASSYRIA

R. Tigris

SYRIA

MEDITERRANEAN SEA

Byblos

R. Euphrates

PALESTINE

Gaza

Memphis

SINAI

ARABIAN DESERT

WESTERN DESERT

EGYPT IN 1450 BC

Under Egypt's direct control

Under Egyptian influence

Thebes

RED SEA

NUBIA

EASTERN DESERT

Buhen

Napata

The warrior Pharaohs of the New Kingdom extended Egypt's empire and influence. Egypt's influence then stretched from the river Euphrates in the north, right down to the Fourth Cataract of the Nile in the south.

Scale: 0 200 400 600 Km / 0 200 400 Miles

▲ Egyptian soldiers used bows and arrows, axes, maces, swords, daggers and curved scimitars as well as long spears and shields.

In the early days, the Egyptian army was small. Its job was to keep out wandering bands of nomads and to protect mining and trading expeditions. Later the army grew in size, because the Egyptians had conquered Nubia in order to gain more trade.

Then Egypt itself was invaded by people known as the Hyksos. The Egyptians were so angry and humiliated by this that they chased the Hyksos out. Then they also set out to capture lands over their eastern frontier, so that these people should never again threaten Egypt. Many other peoples also wanted to rule these lands and eventually the Egyptians had to withdraw.

▼ The Egyptians built fortresses in Nubia as strong as any castle of medieval Europe.

Once, all Egyptian soldiers had fought on foot. But the Hyksos brought a revolutionary new weapon to Egypt. This was the horse and chariot. So Egyptians had to learn to handle horses and fight from chariots.

Some tombs contain pictures of Egyptian troops attacking enemy strongholds. From these we learn that the army used scaling ladders and battering rams.

In the New Kingdom, army officers often became rich and powerful. But a scribe called Khety warned the soldier that he might be killed or horribly wounded. If not, the expenses of his horses, chariot and servants would be so great that he would end his days begging!

▲ A nobleman of the Middle Kingdom placed these models of his soldiers in his tomb. After the conquest of Nubia, many soldiers had to do garrison duty there.

In early times, soldiers wore no armour. Later, they wore leather garments covered with metal scales.

33

Traders and trade

The Egyptians did not have money as we know it. Trading was done by barter, that is by exchanging goods of equal value. This can be a difficult system. It therefore became the custom to decide how much articles were worth in terms of copper weights called deben. You could then exchange articles worth the same amount of copper, or you could give the copper itself.

Individual merchants brought back some goods from abroad but it was the king who sent out important trading missions, such as those which went to Punt. The king also organized the mining expeditions that went to Sinai for copper, turquoise and eye-paint.

Trading expeditions over land often had a strong escort of soldiers. All the goods and supplies that would be needed were carried on the backs of donkeys.

The Egyptians built large and graceful ships to trade with lands across the seas. From early times, Egyptian fleets journeyed regularly to the area now known as the Lebanon. Here the Egyptians bought wood from the great forests and silver from the mines of western Asia.

Pottery
Metal goods
CRETE
MEDITERRANEAN
LIBYA

This map shows some of the goods which Egypt imported. It also shows what Egypt exported in exchange. By conquering Nubia, Egypt got control of the gold mines there. She could then pay foreign countries in gold. One foreign king asked the king of Egypt to send him "gold, gold, and more gold" because in Egypt "gold is as common as dust"

▶ This model is a modern reconstruction of one of the great trading ships which went to Punt in the time of Queen Hatshepsut.

▶ Incense was extremely valuable. Queen Hatshepsut sent an expedition to Punt to bring back incense trees. She hoped to make them grow in Egypt.

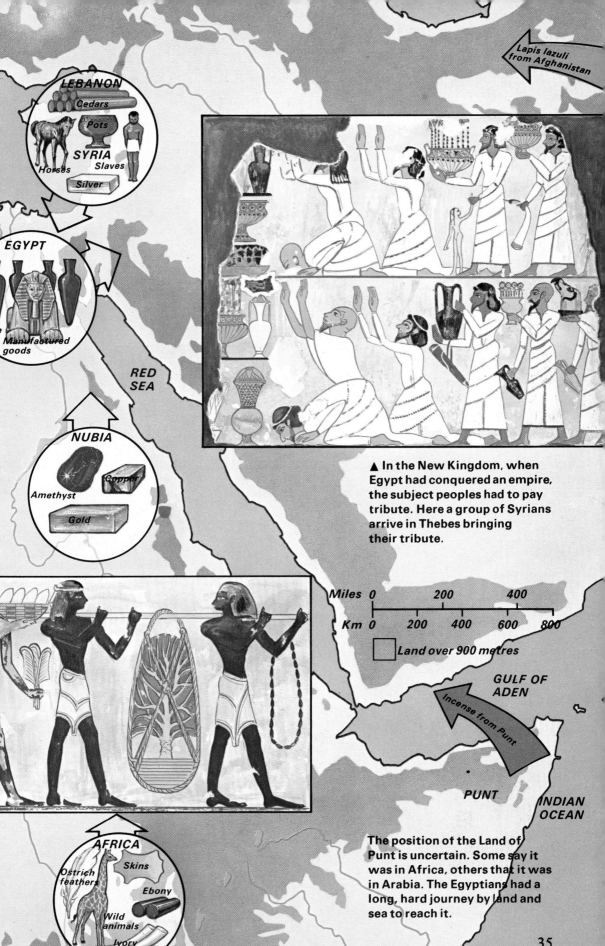

LEBANON
Cedars
Pots
SYRIA
Horses
Slaves
Silver

Lapis lazuli from Afghanistan

EGYPT
Wine
Manufactured goods

RED SEA

NUBIA
Amethyst
Copper
Gold

▲ In the New Kingdom, when Egypt had conquered an empire, the subject peoples had to pay tribute. Here a group of Syrians arrive in Thebes bringing their tribute.

Miles 0   200   400
Km 0   200   400   600   800

Land over 900 metres

GULF OF ADEN

Incense from Punt

PUNT

INDIAN OCEAN

The position of the Land of Punt is uncertain. Some say it was in Africa, others that it was in Arabia. The Egyptians had a long, hard journey by land and sea to reach it.

AFRICA
Ostrich feathers
Skins
Ebony
Wild animals
Ivory

35

Scribes and scrolls

▶ Letters of the hieroglyphic alphabet. The sounds they stand for are above them. But hieroglyphs, the Egyptian system of picture writing, made use of hundreds of signs. A picture might represent one letter, or two or more letters, or even a whole word.

In the inscription below, for example, the signs read: 1-3 = Tut (Image); 4 = ankh (Life); 5-7 = Amun (the god). So we have Tutankhamun, meaning "The Living Image of Amun".

8 = Ruler, 9 = Southern and 10 = On (the name of Thebes). So 8-10 read: "Ruler of Southern On".

Hieroglyphs ceased to be used about AD 400. No-one could read them again until the early 19th century. Then a Frenchman, Champollion, translated them, using the Rosetta Stone. This has the same text written in both Greek and hieroglyphs.

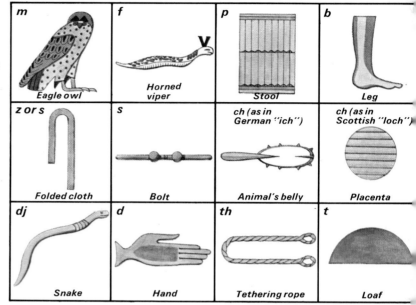

m	*f*	*p*	*b*
Eagle owl	Horned viper	Stool	Leg
z or s	*s*	*ch (as in German "ich")*	*ch (as in Scottish "loch")*
Folded cloth	Bolt	Animal's belly	Placenta
dj	*d*	*th*	*t*
Snake	Hand	Tethering rope	Loaf

▲ A cartouche is an oval frame in which the Egyptians wrote the names of kings.

Learning to write

"A boy's ears are in his back, and he listens when he is beaten!" It seems that learning to write could be a painful business in Egypt, but the results were worth it. "Behold, there is no scribe who lacks for food." These words are taken from a text that school masters made their pupils copy again and again. The author of the text claimed that the job of a scribe was "greater than any other office". Efficient government in Egypt certainly relied on the labours of an army of scribes.

Papyrus scrolls

Papyrus scrolls may seem fragile, but an amazing number have survived in the hot, dry sand of Egypt. Their contents are varied. We have popular stories, like the one telling of the adventures of a man called Sinuhe. We can read letters, like those written by a fussy old priest called Hekanakhte, who lived around 2000 BC.

Scrolls record the Egyptians' mastery of mathematics, which enabled them to build the pyramids. The scrolls also reveal the skill that made Egyptian doctors famous. We can learn of the Egyptians' gods and their studies of the stars. These studies enabled them to calculate their calendar of 365 days, on which ours is based. It was their scholars who divided the day into 24 hours. Thus the scrolls give a glimpse of Egyptian life and learning.

► In Cairo today some Egyptians make papyrus-paper as the ancient Egyptians used to.

v	This sound does not exist in English	i	ah
Quail chick	Arm	Reed	Egyptian vulture
	h	r	n
Twisted flax	Reed shelter	Mouth	Water
k	q	sh	
Stand	Basket	Hill slope	Pool

► Scribes wrote on scrolls of papyrus in black and red inks. To work, they sat cross-legged like this statue.

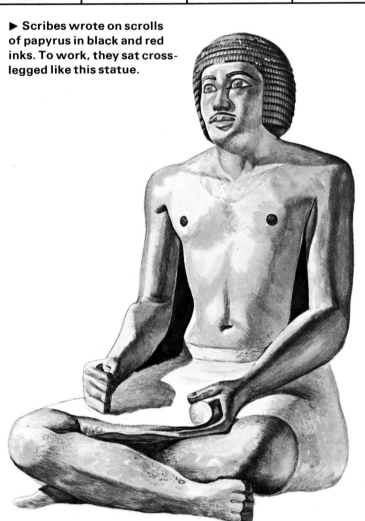

▲ To make papyrus, you remove the green coat of the rush and cut the stem in strips.

▲ To make the sheet, you place a horizontal layer of strips over a vertical layer.

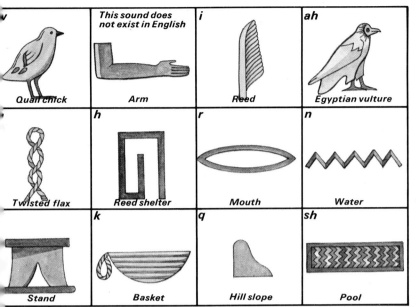

▲ You then pound the sheet to make the strips stick together.

▲ The sheet is then rolled. You now have a thin, smooth sheet, ready for use.

Egyptian craftsmen

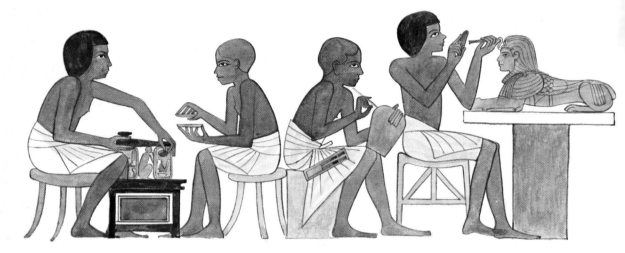

Skilled craftsmen and their training

The vast majority of ancient Egyptians were farmers, but there was always an important minority who were craftsmen. The most skilled were employed by the king, by the temples, or by noblemen who had workshops on their estates. However, there must have been others who worked quietly in small towns and villages, producing things for the local markets.

The sons of craftsmen were expected to follow the same profession as their fathers and to be trained by them. A boy would start training very early. He had to gain skill with his tools which were of copper, bronze or stone with wooden handles. He also had to learn the many rules of his craft.

Strict rules for painters and sculptors

Painters and sculptors in particular had to obey very strict rules. They had to draw everything to the right proportions, and only show people in certain poses. This was because a picture in a tomb was expected to "come alive" in the next world, when the priests had said the right prayers and spells. The scenes shown would then go on happening for all eternity.

If a dead man's body was damaged or destroyed, his spirit might need to pass into a statue of himself. Statues therefore had to show people as they wanted to be for ever—young, strong and handsome. This placed a great responsibility on the craftsmen. A mistake by them might harm their client for ever in the next world.

▲ One of the most beautiful objects made by Egyptian craftsmen is the funeral mask of Tutankhamun. It is made of pure gold and is inlaid with semi-precious stones and coloured glass. It was placed over the face of the dead king.

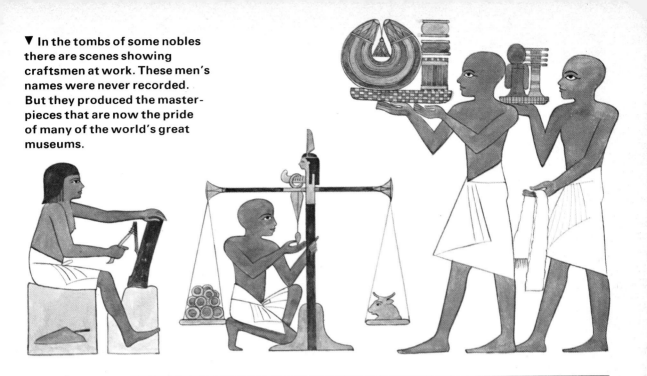

▼ In the tombs of some nobles there are scenes showing craftsmen at work. These men's names were never recorded. But they produced the masterpieces that are now the pride of many of the world's great museums.

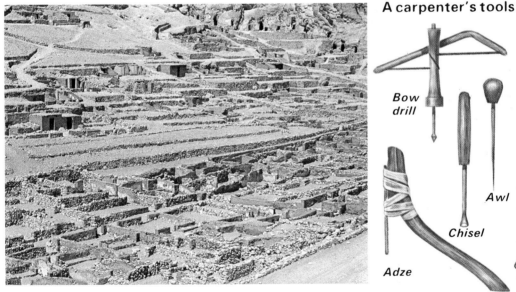

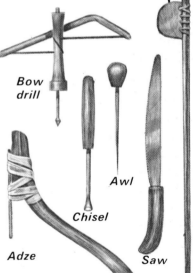

A carpenter's tools

Axe

Bow drill

Awl

Chisel

Adze

Saw

▲ This is how the village known as Deir el Medina looks today. It is situated on the west bank of the Nile at Thebes, and it was the home of the men who made the royal tombs. Generations of men and their families lived in this hot, dry valley.

Modern archaeology has revealed many details about the lives of the workmen in the village of Deir el Medina. They were organized in gangs. Each gang worked for ten days and then had a holiday. A work day was eight hours long, with a break for a rest and a meal. But, according to the records, some men took extra time off.

The workmen were paid for their labours in food, wine, oil and clothing. It sometimes happened that these goods did not arrive on time. Then the men went on strike. They would sit at the gates of a temple and refuse to move till they were paid!

Building pyramids and temples

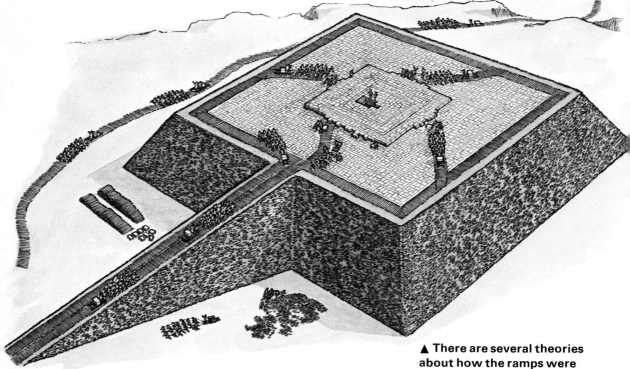

▲ There are several theories about how the ramps were arranged when a pyramid was built. This reconstruction shows one suggestion. Building pyramids required great engineering skill and hard labour.

The Egyptians had no cranes or pulleys. All their monuments were erected by using ramps of rubble and sand. Teams of men dragged the blocks up these. Rollers were sometimes placed under the blocks to make them move more easily. Blocks were laid one layer at a time.

The pyramids at Giza were the largest and most carefully built of all the pyramids. Large blocks of stone were used throughout. The outer casing was of blocks of finest white limestone. Later pyramids were smaller. Some of them had small blocks of stone and rubble inside, while others had only mud bricks. The Giza pyramids are very well preserved.

To build a temple, the Egyptians marked the plan on the ground. Then they laid in position the column bases and the first layer of blocks for the walls. The spaces between the blocks were filled with sand, giving a flat surface over which to pull the next layer of stones.

An ever-growing ramp was used, up which the blocks were dragged. When each layer was in place, more sand was added to give a flat surface again. This went on until the roof was in place. The sand was then removed and decorations could be completed at the same time. The diagrams on page 41 show this method of building.

▲ Stone for building was transported by river. The best limestone came from Tura, near modern Cairo. Granite came from Aswan.

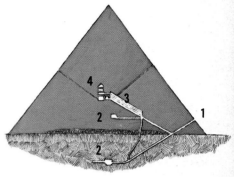

◄ Egypt has some 30 pyramids. This is the pyramid of Chephren, with the Sphinx, at Giza.

▲ Interior of the Great Pyramid of Cheops. 1. Entrance. 2. Unfinished chambers. 3. Grand corridor. 4. Burial chamber.

◄ Part of the temple of Karnak, dedicated to Amun. Many Pharaohs enlarged it, some-times destroying the work of former kings. It was approached by an avenue of ram-headed sphinxes. It contained vast courtyards and lofty halls of columns.

▼ An artist's reconstruction of three stages in the erection of a temple.

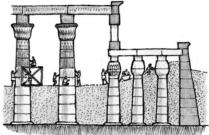

Homes of the gods

The Egyptians believed that there were many gods and goddesses, who took care of all their needs. But for centuries the most powerful was thought to be Amun. There were numerous priests, priestesses, dancers and singers serving these many deities. The gods owned vast estates and great workshops, just like human noblemen.

Egyptian temples, the homes of the gods, all had the same basic plan. You entered through a lofty gateway and passed into one or more wide, open courtyards. Behind these was a vast hall of tall columns, all painted and decorated. The sanctuary was at the far end. Here the divine statue was kept in a shrine. Every day priests made offerings of food, clothing and incense to the god.

Ordinary people were not allowed inside the temples. But the priests could take messages in to the god, begging for help and advice. At certain festivals, the divine statue was put in a small, golden boat, and was carried through the streets by the priests.

Plan of a temple

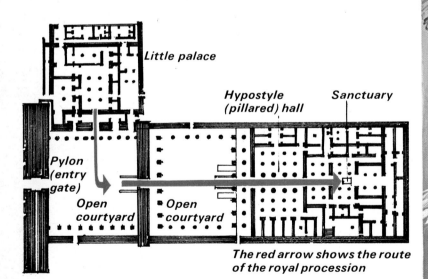

Little palace

Hypostyle (pillared) hall

Sanctuary

Pylon (entry gate)

Open courtyard

Open courtyard

The red arrow shows the route of the royal procession

▲ A plan of Medinet Habu temple. It had a small palace at one side. A royal procession would pass from there, through the courtyards and the column-ed hall to the sanctuary.

▶ Daily, at dawn, the priests and priestesses approached the sanctuary to rouse the god for the new day. On special festivals, the king himself made offerings at the service.

42

Mummies and burial rites

▲ One of the last rituals before burial. Priests hold the coffins, on which holy water is sprinkled. One widow heaps dust on her head.

▼ Shabtis are magical statues of servants who were to do the heavy work in the next world.

The Egyptians used to tell a story about the god Osiris. He had once ruled Egypt as its king and had been murdered by his jealous brother, Set. After many adventures, Isis, the wife of Osiris, managed to restore him to life. The Egyptians believed that, because of this, they too would live after death, in a land ruled by Osiris.

The Egyptians believed that they would have to pass certain tests, to show that they had lived a good life on earth. Then the Fields of the Blessed would be open to them. There they would live a life very like the one which they had known in Egypt, but even more comfortable and free from all troubles.

To enjoy the next life properly, the Egyptians needed food, drink and the possessions they had had on earth. They therefore put all these things in their tombs. If the right prayers and spells were said, these things were supposed to last forever. The Egyptians also painted their tombs with pictures of the good things of this world, so that these would go on happening in the next.

The dead man would need his body, so this was carefully preserved by the process known as mummification. Thanks to this custom, it is now possible to see what ancient Egyptians looked like, and even to find out what diseases they had.

▼ At certain times in their history, the Egyptians also mummified many birds and mammals and buried them like human beings.

▲ With X-rays, you can examine a mummy without disturbing the bandages. X-rays show the state of the body and any jewels among the bindings.

▼ The X-rays of this mummy showed that there was a statue between its legs. Archaeologists carefully cut through the bandages and found a shabti.

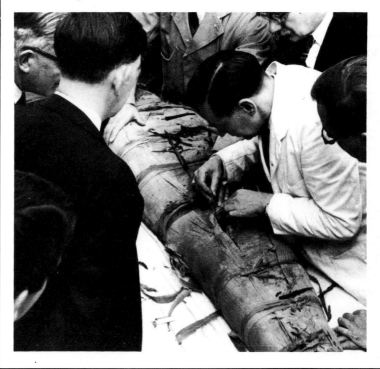

Rock-cut tombs of Thebes

The kings of the Old and Middle Kingdoms had been buried under pyramids, but robbers had broken into every one. King Tuthmosis I therefore decided to hide his tomb. He chose a remote valley at Thebes, above which towered a rocky peak, shaped rather like a pyramid. For over four hundred years the Pharaohs were buried in this valley, in tombs cut deep into the rock by groups of trusted workmen.

When the king was finally laid to rest, surrounded by all the things he would need in the next world, the door was closed. No-one was supposed to enter again. But it was known that treasure was buried there and cunning thieves found the tombs. While robbing the tombs, they sometimes destroyed the bodies of the kings.

Some priests eventually collected the surviving bodies and buried them secretly in other hiding places. These mummies were only found again about a hundred years ago. They have now been removed to Cairo Museum for safe keeping and you can see them there today.

Only one royal tomb escaped the thieves. This was the tomb of Tutankhamun, which was discovered by Howard Carter. It was one of the smallest tombs in the royal valley. It had been hidden by stone chippings when another tomb had been excavated close to it.

▲ The head of King Seti I of the Nineteenth Dynasty. This is one of the best preserved of the royal mummies.

Burial chamber

▲ The rock-cut tomb of Seti I is one of the largest and most splendid in the Valley. Like all the royal tombs, it is decorated. There are pictures of things the king will see in the next world and spells to help him against any danger he may meet. He is also shown being welcomed by the gods.

Entrance from the Valley of the Kings

▲ The Valley of the Tombs of the Kings on the west bank at Thebes, burial place of most of the kings of the New Kingdom.

Well (perhaps to make robbers think it led to the tomb or to drain away any flood water)

▶ The burial chamber of Seti I. The paintings are still rich in colour, though they are over 3000 years old.

Life after death

▼ The Book of the Dead was placed in tombs to guide the dead man through the dangers and difficulties that awaited him in the next world. This picture is from the book of Ani.

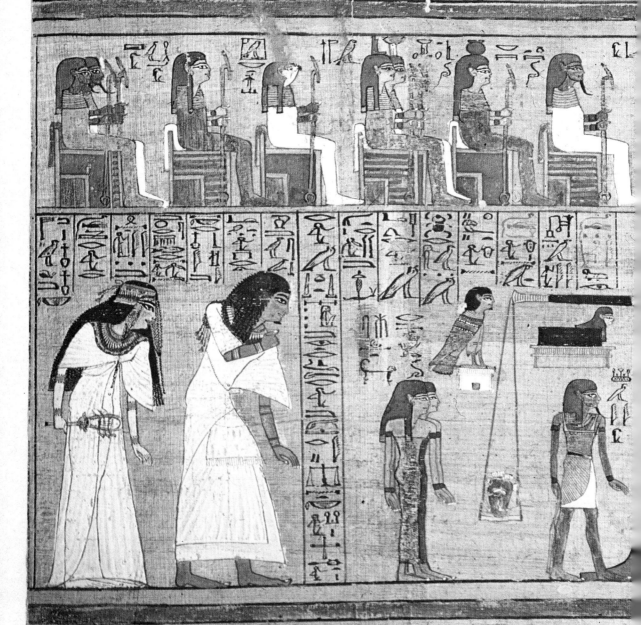

▲ The dead man had to be able to swear that he had not committed any sins. The gods and goddesses, who would sit in judgement on his soul, are across the top of the page.

▲ The dead man and his wife are introduced into the hall of judgement. The trial would take place before Osiris, who is usually shown with his wife, Isis, and his sister.

▲ Anubis, the god with the head of a jackal, guarded the dead. Here he prepares to weigh the heart of the dead man against a feather, which represents Truth.

The Egyptians believed that when they died they entered the kingdom of the god Osiris. There they had to face a trial to decide whether they had led a good life on earth. The virtuous were rewarded by eternal happiness, but a fearful punishment awaited the wicked.

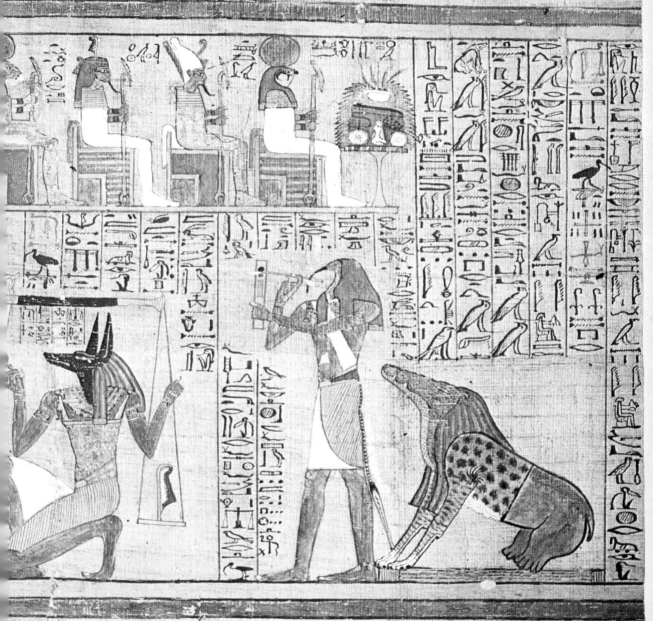

If the heart and the feather were of equal weight, the man had been virtuous during his life. If the heart was heavier than the feather, he had been wicked.

▲ Thoth, who is shown with the head of an ibis, was the god of wisdom. He acted as the scribe of the gods, and wrote down the verdict of their court of judgement.

▲ If the dead man was found guilty of leading a wicked life, this horrible monster was waiting to eat him up! The innocent passed on to a happy existence for ever.

49

The story of Egypt (1)

So long ago that we are not sure of the date, Stone Age people, whose hunting grounds were slowly turning to desert, moved into the Nile Valley. Over the centuries they learned to become farmers and to dig irrigation canals to control the Inundations. The dates in the following story of Egypt are approximate.

▲ Hunters move into the Nile Valley.

?–3200 BC

The Predynastic Period
For generations people lived in small villages, each with its own chief and its gods. They could not write, but we know something about their lives from their remains. Gradually communities united until there were only two kingdoms: Upper and Lower Egypt.

3200–2680 BC

The Archaic Period *Dynasties I and II*
A king of Upper Egypt called Menes conquered Lower Egypt. He ruled his united land from the new capital he built at Memphis. Writing had only just been invented, so there are few inscriptions but we do know the names of the kings. They were buried under rectangular brick tombs at Abydos and Saqqara. It is clear from the remains of goods in these graves that the monarchs were wealthy.

2680–2180 BC

The Old Kingdom *Dynasties III to VI*
Egypt achieved new greatness and this is reflected in the monuments of the god-kings. King Zoser, for example, built the world's first great stone monument. This was his tomb, the Step Pyramid at Saqqara. Later kings built true pyramids at other sites. The greatest of all were those erected at Giza.

The courtiers were buried in rectangular stone tombs called mastabas which were built around pyramids. But some nobles chose to be buried in tombs in the cliffs of the areas where they lived and governed.

Trade flourished with Byblos, Punt and Nubia and Egyptians visited mines in Sinai. Egypt was powerful and prosperous. The craftsmen and artists produced magnificent objects.

▲ Zoser inspects the Step Pyramid.

2180–2130 BC

The First Intermediate Period
Dynasties VII to X
At the end of the Sixth Dynasty rival kings appeared and civil war broke out. Government was weak and ineffective, and people suffered terribly.

2130–1630 BC

The Middle Kingdom

Dynasties XI to XIII

During the civil wars the local princes, known as nomarchs, became very powerful. Then Mentuhotep, the ruler of Thebes, managed to bring the whole land under his control. His family ruled from Thebes and were buried there.

The next family to rule, though they too came from the south, preferred to rule from the area of Memphis. Their pyramids, mostly built around the Faiyum, were not as large as those of the Old Kingdom. The later ones were made of mud brick and only had a stone casing.

All the kings of this, the Twelfth Dynasty, were either named Amenemhet or Senusret. Their favourite god was Amun. When they became rulers of Egypt, they encouraged his worship.

All the old trade links with Punt and the Lebanon were re-established, and mining expeditions flocked to Sinai. Nubia became so important to Egypt that the Egyptians decided to make it an Egyptian province. Several hard campaigns were fought to bring it under Egyptian control. Then fortresses were built there to keep the Nubians in order.

▲ An Egyptian fortress in Nubia.

1630–1560 BC

The Second Intermediate Period

Dynasties XIV to XVII

While the kings of the Middle Kingdom were strong and ruled well, Egypt prospered and her culture flourished. Gradually, however, during the Thirteenth Dynasty, the authority of the kings weakened. Disputes broke out, and then there was a disaster. People from across the eastern frontier took advantage of Egypt's weakness and invaded. These people are known as the Hyksos.

▲ The Hyksos are defeated.

The Hyksos took control of the northern part of Egypt and formed an alliance with the Nubians, who had regained their independence. The southern part of Egypt managed to keep its independence, but tribute had to be paid to the Hyksos.

The Hyksos adopted Egyptian ways and gods and probably ruled very well. But the shame of the Hyksos invasion was so great that the Egyptians never forgot or forgave them.

It was the princes of Thebes who led the struggle for independence against the Hyksos. The fighting went on for several years, but at last the Hyksos were chased from Egyptian soil.

The story of Egypt (2)

1560–1085 BC

The New Kingdom
Dynasties XVIII to XX

A new spirit gripped the Egyptians. It was not enough just to drive the Hyksos out. The Egyptians wanted to wipe out the memory of recent disgrace by conquering other peoples. The horse and chariot had only recently been introduced into Egypt, but the pharaohs and the nobles eagerly trained themselves so that they could use this new weapon.

A succession of warrior pharaohs conquered a vast empire that stretched from the river Euphrates in the north to the Fourth Cataract of the Nile in the south. Trade, tribute and loot brought great wealth into Egypt. Some of this was buried with the kings in their tombs at Thebes.

Mighty temples were built for the god Amun, the King of the Gods, who was thought to be giving the Egyptians their victories. Amun and his priests became very powerful. But one pharaoh, Akhenaten, was inspired by the idea that there was only one god, Aten, the sun disc.

Akhenaten built a new capital for himself at Tell el Amarna. But Tutankhamun moved back to Thebes and re-introduced the worship of Amun and the other gods.

Akhenaten had been so busy with his religious reforms that he had little time for other matters. The Hittites managed to get control of many provinces of the Egyptian empire. A new dynasty, the Nineteenth, replaced the family of Akhenaten on the throne. Two kings, Seti I and Ramesses II, did much to restore Egypt's prestige, but even they could not recover all the provinces that had been lost.

▲ Akhenaten's name is cut from his monuments after his death.

Seti and Ramesses built many temples and cities, and they transferred the capital to the Delta. Thebes, however, remained powerful as the centre of the worship of Amun, and the kings were still buried there in the royal valley.

The Nineteenth Dynasty collapsed as rival princes struggled for the throne. The next family to rule produced only one great warrior pharaoh, Ramesses III.

Ramesses III defeated both the army and the navy of the Philistines and their allies, the Peoples of the Sea, when they attacked Egypt. He thus saved his country's culture and whole way of life. Eight kings ruled after him, all called Ramesses. Most of them were weak rulers and control of affairs passed into the hands of their ministers and priests.

▲ A pharaoh prepares for battle.

▲ The Egyptian fleet has to defeat the Peoples of the Sea.

1085–716 BC

The Third Intermediate Period
Dynasties XXI to XXIV

The documents that survive from this era tell a sad story of high prices, strikes and crime. Rival kings ruled from different cities. For years thieves had been robbing the royal tombs and little could be done to stop them. The situation was so desperate that the priests gathered up the remaining royal mummies and buried them together in secret hiding places.

Not surprisingly, while Egypt was so weak and divided, her empire was lost for ever. Her prestige among nations sank very low. The Hebrew prophet, Isaiah, warned his people against an alliance with Egypt, because it was a "broken reed".

716–332 BC

The Late Period
Dynasties XXV to XXXI

During the Twenty-fifth and Twenty-sixth Dynasties, Egypt enjoyed a new era of peace and prosperity. But her independence was doomed. First the Assyrians, then the Persians conquered Egypt, although several Egyptian kings made gallant efforts to keep them out.

332–30 BC

The Ptolemaic Period

The Egyptians welcomed the arrival of Alexander, called the Great, of Macedon, because he drove out the Persians. Egypt became part of his empire, but the empire was destined to die with him a few years later. Alexander had left one of his generals, Ptolemy, in Egypt.

Ptolemy became Pharaoh, founding a line of kings and queens who ruled Egypt for three hundred years. The last of these was the famous Cleopatra. She supported Mark Antony in the civil wars in Rome after the murder of Julius Caesar.

Antony and Cleopatra were defeated by Octavius Caesar, who later became the Emperor Augustus. Egypt became a Roman province. Cleopatra, the last ruler of an independent Egypt, committed suicide rather than be taken prisoner.

▲ After the defeat of Cleopatra Egypt submits to Rome.

Though Cleopatra was a Macedonian, and not an Egyptian, she was a worthy successor of the great pharaohs of Egypt. Her name has always been remembered. As the Egyptians themselves said: "A man is perished, his corpse is dust, all his relatives are come to the ground, but writing makes him remembered".

Famous Egyptians

Menes was, according to tradition, the king who united Egypt and founded the First Dynasty. Unfortunately we do not know for certain which of the kings is to be identified as Menes, but he may have been Narmer. Menes is supposed to have founded the city of Memphis. Manetho (see below) tells us he was killed by a hippopotamus.

Imhotep was the chief minister of King Zoser of the Third Dynasty. He was one of those extremely clever people who are very good at several different things. He was the architect who designed the Step Pyramid, and tradition says he was also a scholar and a doctor. His reputation for wisdom was so great that in the Late Period he was worshipped as a god.

Hetepheres (Fourth Dynasty) was the mother of Cheops. Archaeologists found her tomb and its furniture where it had been hidden by her son, but her body was missing.

Cheops, Chephren and Mycerinus were kings of the Fourth Dynasty. They built the greatest of all the pyramids, those at Giza.

Unas was the last king of the Fifth Dynasty. The burial chamber of his pyramid was the first to be inscribed with spells known as the Pyramid Texts.

Pepi II (Sixth Dynasty) had the longest known reign in history. He was six years old when he became king and lived to be one hundred. His pyramid was called Men nefer Pepi, and the name of Memphis is derived from this.

Harkhuf led trading expeditions to Nubia in the reign of Pepi II. Once he brought home a dancing pygmy, to the delight of the boy king.

▲ A statue of King Chephren.

Nebhepetre Mentuhotep (Eleventh Dynasty) was a prince of Thebes. He was responsible for uniting Egypt after the First Intermediate Period.

Senusret III was a great pharaoh of the Twelfth Dynasty who managed to reduce the power of the nomarchs and to re-organize the government. He was a brilliant general and strengthened the defences of the forts in Nubia.

Teti-sheri (Seventeenth Dynasty) was a commoner but many of Egypt's great kings were among her descendants. Her son and grandson died in the struggle against the Hyksos. However, she lived long enough to see the victories of her other grandson, Ahmose.

Ineni was architect to King Tuthmosis I of the Eighteenth Dynasty. He chose the remote valley at Thebes where so many royal tombs were later hidden.

Hatshepsut (Eighteenth Dynasty) seized the throne on the death of her half-brother, Tuthmosis II, who was also her husband. She had a long and prosperous reign and sent a very famous expedition to Punt for incense trees. Her architect, Senenmut, designed a superb temple for her at Deir el Bahari.

Tuthmosis III nephew of Hatshepsut and the greatest of all the warrior kings of the Eighteenth Dynasty. He extended the empire to its widest limits.

Rekhmire was the Vizier of Tuthmosis III. His tomb is one of the most impressive of the tombs of the nobles. A long inscription in the tomb tells of his duties and heavy responsibilities.

Nefertiti (Eighteenth Dynasty) was the wife of Akhenaten and he loved her very dearly. Her portrait, found at Tell el Amarna, shows that she was an extremely lovely woman. Many scenes survive showing her and her family worshipping Aten.

Tutankhamun (Eighteenth Dynasty) married one of the daughters of Akhenaten and Nefertiti. He was only nine when he came to the throne and he reigned for less than ten years. But he is the most famous of all the pharaohs because his tomb is the only one that was not robbed in antiquity.

Ramesses II (Nineteenth Dynasty) fought many wars against the Hittites, but his most famous battle was at Kadesh. He built the great temple of Abu Simbel, and many other temples and cities. He may have been pharaoh when the Israelites fled from Egypt. He had many wives, but his favourite was Nefertari. He built a small temple for her at Abu Simbel and a splendidly decorated tomb in the Valley of the Queens. He reigned for 67 years.

Ramesses III (Twentieth Dynasty) was the pharaoh who saved Egypt from invasion by the Peoples of the Sea. We can read about his victories in the inscription on the walls of his impressive temple of Medinet Habu. His reign ended in tragedy. One of his wives plotted to make her son king, instead of the chosen heir. Documents still survive telling of the trial that followed.

Manetho was an Egyptian priest who lived early in the Ptolemaic Period. He wrote a great history of Egypt, based on records long since destroyed. In his book, he divided Egypt's kings into groups or dynasties. So far, no copy of his book has been found. We know about it from the works of other authors, who quoted passages from it in their books.

▲ Queen Nefertiti, wife of Akhenaten.

Ancient Egypt

Egypt is a very narrow country for most of its length. It only widens out in the Faiyum and the Delta. Apart from the Mediterranean coast, Egypt is entirely surrounded by deserts. The Egyptians called the desert the Red Land and the cultivated land the Black Land.

In six places the Nile is full of huge rocks, which make it difficult for ships to pass. These are the cataracts.

To improve the supply of water and make farming more efficient, the modern Egyptians have built the High Dam at Aswan. This has caused a huge lake to form behind it, which has drowned Nubia. However, the Egyptian government and archaeologists from all over the world have managed to save temples like those at Abu Simbel and Philae.

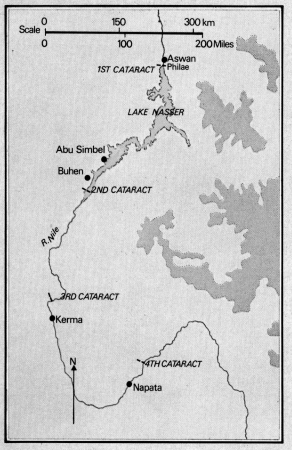

A map of the Nile from Aswan south to the Fourth Cataract.

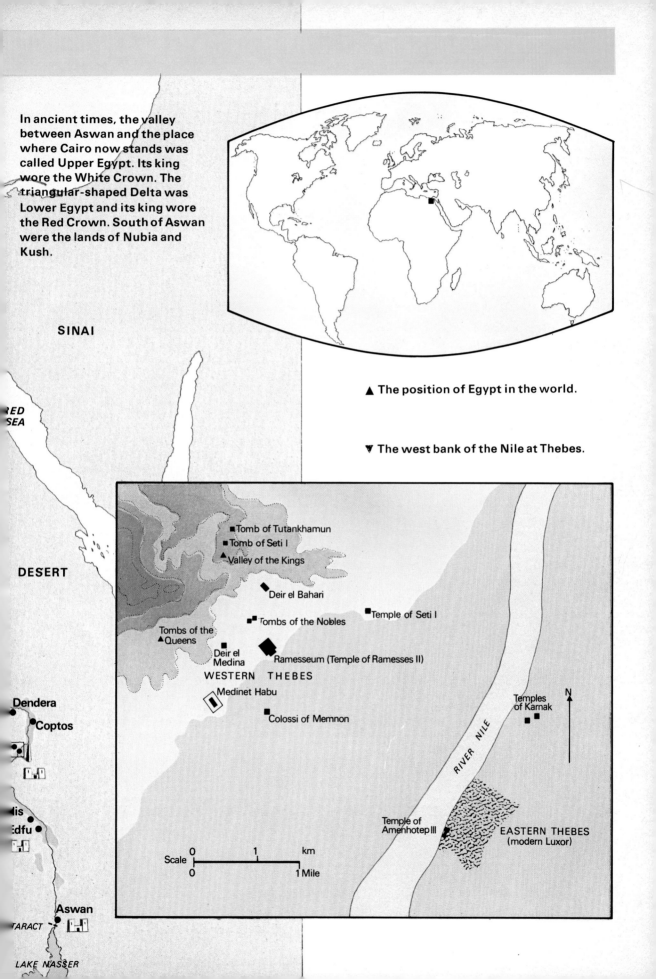

In ancient times, the valley between Aswan and the place where Cairo now stands was called Upper Egypt. Its king wore the White Crown. The triangular-shaped Delta was Lower Egypt and its king wore the Red Crown. South of Aswan were the lands of Nubia and Kush.

SINAI

RED SEA

DESERT

▲ The position of Egypt in the world.

▼ The west bank of the Nile at Thebes.

■ Tomb of Tutankhamun
■ Tomb of Seti I
▲ Valley of the Kings
◆ Deir el Bahari
■ Temple of Seti I
■ Tombs of the Nobles
Tombs of the ▲ Queens
■ Deir el Medina
◆ Ramesseum (Temple of Ramesses II)
WESTERN THEBES
▱ Medinet Habu
■ Colossi of Memnon

Dendera
Coptos

RIVER NILE

Temples of Karnak

N

Temple of Amenhotep III
EASTERN THEBES (modern Luxor)

is
Edfu

Scale
0 — 1 — km
0 — 1 Mile

Aswan
ARACT

LAKE NASSER

World history 3500 BC to AD 1

	Egypt	Europe	Asia
3500 BC	In Predynastic Egypt, the people are making pottery and stone vessels. They have learnt to use metals and to weave. By the time Egypt is united in about 3200, they have also invented a system of writing. The Archaic Period. Beginnings of the Old Kingdom period.	Europe is populated by farmers, who use stone tools and make pottery. Many tribes migrate right across Europe before the Roman Empire is established. They take their distinctive cultures with them. Archaeologists can trace their routes through their pottery, burial customs and metal work.	In the Yellow River basin in China there are farming communities. They use stone tools and make pottery. In India, in the Indus Valley, a more advanced, metal-using culture is established. They trade with Mesopotamia.
2800 BC	The Pyramid Age, when all the great pyramids are built for the Old Kingdom monarchs. Regular trade with Byblos, Punt, Nubia and Sinai. 2180-2130. The First Intermediate Period. Civil wars split Egypt and the nomarchs greatly increase their power. The Middle Kingdom.	The rise of the Minoan civilization in Crete. It evolves its own system of writing, independent from those of Egypt and Mesopotamia. Huge stone palaces are built throughout Crete. The most famous of these is Knossos. Trade flourishes with Greece and Asia Minor.	The Indus Valley people build great cities at Mohenjo-daro and Harrapa. They have invented their own system of writing. In the Yellow River basin the people are producing a fine painted pottery.
2100 BC	Egyptian culture flourishes. Conquest of Nubia. Widespread trade. This great era is followed by the Second Intermediate Period, when the Hyksos conquer much of Egypt. Around 1560 Egypt regains her independence. The New Kingdom.	The Beaker People arrive in Britain. The use of metal for tools and weapons is now becoming widespread in Europe. The rise of Mycenae in Greece. Stonehenge completed in Britain. The destruction of Knossos and other Cretan palaces.	In China the legendary Hsia Dynasty are said to have ruled. The Indo-Aryans begin arriving in India and establish themselves in the north-west. The Shang Dynasty is founded in China. People discover how to make bronze.
1400 BC	Egypt conquers a large empire in the near east and regains control of Nubia. The capital is at Thebes and Amun is the state god. This period of greatness lasts for about 500 years. It is followed by the Third Intermediate Period, when Egypt declines as a world power.	The Greeks attack Troy. Invasion of Greece by the Dorians and the destruction of Mycenae. The Etruscan civilization develops in northern Italy. Rome is founded in 753 BC.	The beginnings of a system of writing appear in China. Under the Shang Dynasty very fine ritual vessels of bronze are made. The rulers are buried in great pit tombs. 1027. The Western Chou Dynasty. In India the Aryans begin to take over more and more land. The caste system begins.
700 BC	A short revival of unity and prosperity in the Late Period is followed by defeat and occupation, first by the Assyrians, then by the Persians. In 332 Alexander conquers Egypt. Egypt is ruled by the Ptolemies. Cleopatra commits suicide in 30 BC. Egypt becomes a Roman province.	City states flourish in Greece. 509. Rome becomes a republic. The Greeks successfully hold out against Persian invasions. But then Athens and Sparta fight each other. Alexander conquers Persia and Egypt. 264-146. Rome fights Carthage. 73. Slave revolt of Spartacus. 55/54. Caesar invades Britain.	771. Eastern Chou Dynasty in China. Birth of the Buddha in India and of Confucius in China. The Chinese begin to build the Great Wall. Alexander invades India in 327 BC. 221-206. Ch'in Dynasty in China. China is united under the Han Dynasty in 206 BC.
AD 1			

Africa	Near East	America	
			3500 BC
The peoples of north Africa are in touch with Egypt and the cultures of the Mediterranean. South of the Sahara, however, most people retain their more simple, traditional ways of life. They preserve a Stone Age culture into the Christian era.	As in Egypt, the conditions around the great rivers of Mesopotamia give birth to an advanced civilization at an early date. Pottery, weaving, the use of metals and writing are all known. People live in city states. The First Dynasty of Ur.	In South America, simple farming spreads, combined with food gathering, fishing and hunting. The people use stone tools and do simple weaving.	
			2800 BC
Egypt begins trading regularly with Punt, which may have been on the coast of Somaliland. If the "dancing dwarf" brought to Egypt by Harkhuf was a true pygmy, there must have been trade routes across Africa, though the Egyptians themselves never went so far.	Throughout the Near East, city states grow and flourish. There is regular trade between Byblos and Egypt. Amorites, a Semitic-speaking people, gradually settle in Mesopotamia. Sargon of Agade reigns. The Third Dynasty of Ur.	Improvements in farming. A wider range of plants is grown. Early examples of pottery appear in Colombia and Ecuador.	
			2100 BC
Egypt conquers Nubia. The Kingdom of Kush, centred on the city of Kerma, flourishes in what is now the Sudan. Nubia briefly gains its independence during the Second Intermediate Period. But in the New Kingdom, Nubia and Kush are again part of the Egyptian Empire.	Ur falls just before 2000 BC. Assyrian merchants in Turkey. The First Dynasty of Babylon. The greatest of its rulers is Hammurabi. The rise to power of the Hittite peoples in Turkey. Indo-Europeans appear in the Near East and Kassites rule in Babylon.	Pottery is made in Peru around 2000 BC. A distinctive culture begins to emerge there. Settlement of Mayan peoples in Yucatan.	
			1400 BC
Around 1080 BC Nubia and Kush break away from Egypt and become a separate kingdom. Colonists from Tyre found the city of Carthage in 814 BC. For a few years, Egypt is ruled by Nubian kings, whose capital is Napata.	The Egyptian Empire dominates much of the Near East. About 1200 the Peoples of the Sea cause turmoil throughout the entire area. One tribe, the Peleset (Philistines) settle and give their name to Palestine. David and Solomon reign around 1013-933 BC. Rise of the Assyrian Empire.	Rise of the Olmec culture of Mexico around 1200 BC onwards. Chavín di Huántar, a settlement and ceremonial centre in Peru, is founded around 900 BC. Stone buildings, including pyramids, are erected. First examples of gold ornaments appear in Peru.	
			700 BC
Phoenicians, sent by Pharaoh Necho, may have sailed round Africa around 600 BC. Hanno the Phoenician explores the west coast of Africa in 450 BC. The rise of the kingdom of Meroe in the Sudan. Rome annexes North Africa, having defeated Carthage after long years of war.	The Babylonians destroy Jerusalem in 587 BC. The empire of Nebuchadnezzar. The Persians conquer the entire Near East. Darius I founds Persepolis. The conquests of Alexander. The rise of the Roman Empire.	Development of the Mayan culture. The Zapotec capital of Monte Alban in Mexico is founded around 600 BC. Toltecs settle in Mexico. Writing makes its first appearance in Mexico. A calendar is probably in use.	
			AD 1

Glossary

cataracts places in the Nile where the river is full of rocks.

dynasty Manetho divided the kings of Egypt into groups or dynasties. Each dynasty usually represents an entire royal family, but some families cover two dynasties.

ibis a long-legged wading bird with a long curved bill.

Inundation the flood that used to cover Egypt once a year.

kiosk shelter on roof of house.

Lower Egypt the triangular-shaped Delta region.

mastaba a rectangular building over a tomb. A mastaba might be a solid structure, or it might contain rooms. The burial was at the bottom of a shaft under the mastaba.

mummification the process used to preserve the dead. The internal organs were removed and the body was left for weeks covered by a substance called natron. This helped to preserve it. The body was then wrapped, each limb separately, in many layers of bandages.

nomarch the title given to noblemen who, in the Old and Middle Kingdoms, governed districts of Egypt known as nomes.

obelisk a long shaft of stone, usually very tall, with a pyramid-shaped top.

palette used by the Egyptians for mixing paints, inks and eye-paint.

Peoples of the Sea people who came from the islands of the Mediterranean Sea.

reconstruction an attempt to recreate something as it was in the past. A reconstruction can be a painting or an object.

scarab a sacred beetle.

shabti or **ushabti** small, magical statue buried with dead person to work for him in the next world.

Thebes the name given by the ancient Greeks to the city of Wast. Thebes was on both banks of the river. The part that was on the east bank is covered by modern Luxor.

Upper Egypt the Nile valley between Aswan and the area of modern Cairo.

Index